THE POWER OF HUMANITY

ANYONE CAN SUCCEED USING THIS ANCIENT KNOWLEDGE

Thomas E. Montagu

THE POWER OF HUMANITY
Anyone can succeed using this ancient knowledge.

Written by Thomas E. Montagu

© Copyright 2013 Thomas E. Montagu
ISBN: 978-1490379227

All rights reserved.

No part of this book shall be reproduced, stored in a retrieval system, or transmitted by any means, electronic, mechanical, photocopying, recording, or otherwise without written permission by the author and/or publisher.

There is awesome power in our universe that can be accessed by anyone, anytime, anywhere. All we have to do is understand what it is and how to tap into it. Then we can begin using these amazing, natural forces to enrich our human experience.

To my wife, best friend and life partner Carolyn,

Thank you for believing in me and sharing your love unconditionally.

To our children, our grand children, family and friends;

You all have brought me joy and inspiration. I pray you will discover the abundant happiness, peace and prosperity that you deserve.

My hope is that your natural human curiosity will be the driving force which creates a compelling desire within you to access these ancient secrets and realize all of your dreams.

To everyone else,

I intend to plant the seeds of inspiration for humanity with the hopes that those of you who seek this ancient knowledge will go out and become successful in every way you choose.

Introduction

For thousands of years, many amazing powerful ancient secrets were hidden, guarded and held sacred by great rulers.

Throughout the ages, countless wars were fought, entire cities destroyed and thousands died in bloody battles trying to prevent these powerful ancient secrets from being revealed to the world.

Shockingly, there are still many powerful and influential people in this world who, to this day, do not want you to have access to this powerful ancient knowledge!

Don't let their efforts get in your way!

Don't let them prevent you from reaching for your dreams and achieving your goals!

Be the person you want others to think you are. The Power of Humanity will transform you, your life and the lives of those surrounding you!

Improve relationships, advance your career, build wealth, improve your health…the options are endless! Anyone can use this ancient knowledge to realize their dreams and accomplish amazing goals!

We only need to acknowledge their existence and understand that there are amazing natural forces in the cosmos which "automatically" enhance our efforts to reach higher levels of success.

Everything has its beauty but not everyone sees it.
-Confucius

The more man meditates upon good thoughts the better will be his world & the world at large. -Confucius

A man grows most tired while standing still.
-Chinese Proverbs

You will never know what you're good at until you try.
-Chinese Proverbs

Learning is a treasure that will follow its owner everywhere. -Chinese Proverb

In the end, it's not the years in your life that count. It's the life in your years. -Abraham Lincoln

Do unto others as you would have them do unto you.
-Jesus Christ

All of these words of wisdom speak truth and offer valuable advice. Heed their message and you too will become victorious in your quest for success!

My Mission

To share unconventional ideas and concepts that will inspire and motivate others, helping them to realize their dreams while simultaneously achieving higher levels of performance, happiness and prosperity.

Everything in these pages expresses my personal belief and understanding of the world (s) around us.

Some people will be confused by what is written here, some will think I am nuts, some may be offended with these concepts while others will be enlightened and empowered to seek (and achieve) amazing success in anything they want.

Contents

We All Have to Start Somewhere   11

Discovering the Power of Humanity   23

The Choices We Make   36

The Ancient Secrets   44

The Natural Laws of Expansion   49

Use it or Lose it!   57

Second Chances Are Real!   68

Be ABLE to Use the Power   77

Words of Wisdom from the Masters   91

We All Have to Start Somewhere

Life has a funny way of sneaking up on you. Suffice it to say I spent my younger years focused on "enjoying" the late 1960's and all of the 1970's.

Anyone who lived through the era of hippies, flower power, peace and love knows exactly what I'm talking about.

One of the biggest mistakes I made back then was dropping out of high school in the tenth grade. I was a long haired rebellious teen-ager who thought he knew everything.

It didn't help that my father had passed away when I was 15 and my mother was sick and institutionalized for as long as I can remember. You might say my chances for survival were next to zero.

I was certainly on a path of self destruction in those days, living on the edge, running through the streets of Cleveland, Ohio without a clue of the dangerous road I was traveling down.

I was definitely one of those "least likely to succeed" kids from "the wrong side of the tracks". Trouble was my middle name. Thankfully, those cold, dark days are a complete blur to me now.

There's no need to bore you with all the details so, I won't go into all of the chaotic, selfish, childish and reckless activities that took place back then, on weekends, holidays or any other chance (excuse) I had to do something stupid, that's a story for another time.

I don't know how or why, but somehow, I miraculously survived and climbed out of the black, bottomless pit I had fallen into.

Somehow, I managed to survive those days, eventually ended up getting married, and had two children.

I had begun my quest to achieve "the American dream".

I worked any job I could find (there weren't many) that didn't require a diploma or any skills, moving from state to state, one rental house to another while scratching and clawing my way through young adulthood, eventually ending up divorced and ultimately going bankrupt. Not a stellar participant in society.

Today, my life is very different. I consider myself to be extremely fortunate and successful, even though I don't (currently) have millions of dollars in my pocket or spend my weekends jetting around to exotic places. What I do have is a clear understanding of how, through the realization of The Power of Humanity, it is possible to transcend seemingly insurmountable obstacles and achieve the goals I once perceived impossible.

I have chosen a path which is taking me on an amazing journey, discovering unbelievable happiness and love, gaining knowledge and power along the way. I have realized that chasing the "American dream" is a worthy endeavor, fun and very achievable.

Every day continues to be surprisingly better than the last and my confidence to reach for and do whatever it takes to achieve real results is constantly, naturally growing.

Everything in these pages expresses my personal belief and understanding of the world(s) around us. Some people will be confused by what is written here, some will think I am nuts, some may be offended while others will be enlightened and empowered to seek (and achieve) amazing success in anything they want.

I intend to plant the seeds of inspiration with hopes that those who seek this ancient knowledge will go out and become successful in every way they choose.

Nothing revealed here is revolutionary in content, even though you'll have to do some diligent research, sorting through many books and records to understand just how ancient this secret knowledge really is.

All of my beliefs and advice come from knowledge that has been around as long as human kind, since the beginning of everything.

What I am attempting to do is simply ensure that you have access to abundant power and the same chance to succeed as anyone else on this planet. After all, not everyone has read or heard about these ancient secrets and unfortunately, there *are many people in this world who would like to keep it that way.*

The most important advice I have to offer is that you must learn and read everything and anything you can. Seek information.

There are libraries filled with books available to all of us. Many were written explicitly about ancient cultures, powerful rulers, scientists and inventors. Specific details of what they did and how they did it are at your fingertips.

Seek and you will find!

Have you ever heard of the old cliché "knowledge is power"? Believe me when I say this statement is absolutely true. It is essential and necessary to possess knowledge in order to improve your circumstances.

Simply stated, if you know how to do something, anything, you can master it.

Go forth and do just that! You can and will succeed as long as you have a true desire and are willing to do so.

The key is that you have to go after it and you have to work for it. Nobody can do it for you.

It all started to come together for me when I was honest with myself and realized that I was not happy with my life the way it was. Something was missing.

I knew there had to be a better way somehow. That's when I began to seek an understanding of why things (good or bad) happen and what I could do (if anything) to change them. I kept an open mind, read anything I could get my hands on and listened to what people that fit my vision of success had to say.

It is no secret that there are abundant ways to learn. Many of the successful people we know today are highly educated scholars. There are also many successful people who, like me, learned at the "school of hard knocks".

Experience and self-education, along with a true desire and willingness for change will help propel anyone to magnificent achievements in their lives.

The good news is that you don't have to be a college graduate to be successful. I am proof of that. This doesn't mean you shouldn't go to college. We need Teachers, Scientists, Engineers and Doctors in our world. If you desire to be one and are willing to work for it, you will most likely succeed.

The most important step to take on this journey is to decide what you want to do. This may sound easy but in reality, it is the most difficult part. Once you do decide what you want and where you want to be, you can begin to learn about it, master it and become successful.

Don't wait any longer- get started now!

Sometimes it helps to tap into other people for their knowledge and advice. There is no need to reinvent the wheel when others have already done the leg work! I'll bet you know someone successful that would jump at the chance to help you with any questions you might have. All you have to do is ask.

Books, Newspapers, Magazines Internet & Television are awesome avenues for abundant information as well, so be sure to read, listen and watch everything you can about anything you can, especially what you are passionate about.

Focus your efforts on the subjects that interest you most. I believe that you'll discover along the way exactly what it is you want to do with your life.

One day, out of nowhere, it (the answer) will "magically" come to you. You'll know what you want to do and who you want to be. From there, the sky's the limit!

For me, reading was one invaluable activity in the quest for increasing my chances for success. At first, I read newspapers and magazines mostly and was intrigued with advances in Science, Nature and Technology. I love the natural world and was always fascinated with astronomy.

Stories of building companies, creating wealth and success caught my interest as well. Like everyone I know, I dreamed of one day being rich and famous. (still working on it!)

As a young adult, my only thoughts were about money. I needed money just to survive. It is no secret that food, clothing, shelter, health & security are all essential, basic necessities in life.

It didn't take long for me to realize that I really didn't know anything about making money. Naturally, I defaulted to a simple conclusion. I needed a job.

I didn't know then that there were any real opportunities for me to be one of those highly successful people, so off I went into the working world. After all, as I remember, my father worked hard all of his life and set an example for me.

I believed hard work was the key and hoped that someday it would pay off.

I performed many different jobs over the years, everything from washing dishes to landscaping, painting houses, warehousing, cooking, assembly lines, manufacturing and I even tried selling Kirby vacuum cleaners door to door.

I was an uneducated, inexperienced young kid feeling my way through life, trying to make a buck.

Happiness and success, as far as I could tell, were just a fantasy. I was struggling every day just to survive.

Needless to say, nothing I did in those days seemed like it was worth the time and effort. Work didn't amount to much back then, which was a meager "survival" at best.

Round and round I went spinning my wheels. Wandering aimlessly through life doing as little as possible just to get by and survive until the next day.

I spent most of my free time watching TV and hanging out with "friends" while spending what little cash I did have on useless stuff. Sound familiar?

I can say that one of my most productive time-wasting activities (ironic eh?) was watching TV. This was where I developed my imaginative skills.

Watching programs about nature, history, evolution, space, religion and science fiction enlightened me to the endless possibilities in our universe. It was my "escape" from the day to day drudgery.

I didn't know it then, but that was the catalyst which "opened my mind" and allowed me to accept, understand and embrace the Powers of Humanity later in life.

Somewhere along the way I realized that everything I did to improve my situation actually brought all of my thoughts and dreams within my reach. Because of this, a whole new purpose has emerged for me.

I have a growing desire to share this awesome power with family and friends. If I can be blessed with this knowledge and the results of putting it to use, so can they and so too, can you!

Imagine what it will feel like when you can realize your dreams and transform your life!

I don't want to give the wrong impression here, it took many years for me to finally understand and realize the power of these ancient secrets. Nothing was gained overnight or without serious, tremendous focus and effort.

The amazing thing is that I have arrived at this moment with a clear understanding and belief that better days are still ahead of me and I have the ability to influence the outcome.

My quest for understanding the Power of Humanity continues and this book is a small step on the way of this long, wonderful journey.

Remember that I mentioned earlier that there are powerful people in this world who, to this day, do not want you to have access to these ancient secrets! Don't let their efforts get in your way. Don't let them prevent you from reaching for your dreams and achieving your goals!

My hope is that your natural human curiosity will be a driving force within you which creates a compelling desire for you to access these ancient secrets, discovering The Power of Humanity for yourself.

Discovering the Power of Humanity

I believe we all have had, or most certainly will have the experience of a significant, personal event which will stir something inside us that we really don't understand. We may not even consciously notice that something important has happened at all.

In most cases we will not immediately recognize it as important and certainly not as a "life changing" event. It happens to everyone naturally and if we can remember it or look for it to come in the future, we can use it to help us discover the ancient secrets of The Power of Humanity and begin the journey to amazing success!

One such event occurred in my life that "kick started" my quest for this secret ancient knowledge. I did not recognize it at the time, but my life would be changed forever and the path I traveled (and continue on today) would be renewed with excitement and challenges that were shaping my future.

My journey began when I was a 26 year old factory operator. I was working 12 hour shifts, 7 days a week, struggling to support a wife, two kids, her father, a dog and the occasional brother in law living in a small rental house in Fort Wayne, Indiana.

I was neck deep in hospital bills, credit card debt and barely keeping the old clunker of a car running. Man, I thought "this is the life"! I'm living the "American dream"! I did not know that there could be anything better. It was a normal life, as far as I could tell.

I was working hard, paying out every dime I ever made and wishing for a day off so I could just sleep in a couple of extra hours and then start the cycle all over again, day in and day out, spinning my wheels, round and round. Sound familiar?

One amazing day however, would change everything. It was as if I had just awakened from a long, dark and dreamless sleep. The day before was a blur, just like every other day, simply because I had no idea where I was or where I was headed. I was just getting through each day in survival mode.

It started out innocently, as a normal uneventful day. I woke up on a hot, August morning and was getting ready to take my first trip on an airplane for some company training. This alone may seem inconsequential to most people but for me, it was terrifying!

All my life I have had a *fear* of flying. I don't know why or where it came from, but to me it was real. I can remember on more than one occasion stating that "if I can't get there by car, boat or train, I'm not going".

I had convinced myself that I was happy right where I was, with both feet on the ground. After all, "if a man was supposed to fly he would have been born with wings".

In spite of my fears I had to go on the trip because my job required it. I can tell you that I was not looking forward to this event at all. As I drove to the airport, all I could do was think about all of the terrible things that were going to happen to me, the worst of all would be getting killed in a terrible flaming plane crash! I was so full of anxiety that I felt like I was going to puke.

In spite of my terror, I continued on and headed for the boarding gate. Once there, I met up with my traveling partner, Shirley (not her real name).

She was the secretary who more or less ran the office at the factory where we worked. She too, had a fear of flying that was clearly evident by the look on her face and due to the fact that she was clutching a bible in her hand so tightly that you couldn't have pried it away with a crow bar!

Shirley's anxiety was as intense as mine and clearly evident when she spoke. "I don't want to do this" she mumbled, "I've never been on a plane before". "Me neither", I said, trying to hide my own nervousness, I continued, attempting to reassure her (and myself) "don't worry, it's a short flight, we'll be there before you know it".

Soon, the dreaded boarding process began. As we made our way down the jet-way to the airplane our anxiety continued to grow.

There before us was an old rickety turbo-prop 50 seat "puddle jumper" (If you've ever taken a commuter flight, you know exactly what I mean by "puddle jumper") with the right wing propeller sputtering slowly while the prop on the left wing stayed motionless.

I could not keep myself from wondering why one engine was running without the other. I thought to myself, "With my luck it's probably because they wouldn't be able to get it started again!"

Still, I reluctantly pushed forward towards the plane.

When we climbed up the stairs towards the main cabin, I peered into the cockpit, briefly studying the controls and thinking that they looked oddly simple and familiar.

They reminded me of an old war movie (do you remember the Red Baron?) with 2-seater bi-planes that the pilots controlled with a stick in the floor, their scarves flailing in the wind as they shook their fists at each other during a "dog fight" in the sky.

This was not what I expected to see in there. I mumbled under my breath, "where's all the latest technology"? I thought, "we fly people to outer-space routinely and this is the best I get for my first trip off the ground"?

Sarcastically, I continued under my breath, "wonderful".

While we looked for our seats, I remember it felt like we were stumbling into an old school bus with 2 seats per row and barely enough room for a person to walk down the center aisle.

I kept expecting some stupid kid to stick his foot out so I would trip and fall. Still, I pressed on towards my seat.

I was terribly anxious and my heart was pounding. I was keenly aware of every step. It was like walking across an old rotted wooden floor.

I heard every creak and squeak of the plane as we slowly stumbled through the aisle.

I looked at Shirley as we reached our row. She nervously insisted, "You take the window, I can't bear to look out". "Oh great", I thought, "what makes her think I want to look out"?

I attempted to hide my own reluctant fear as I said "sure" then we buckled in and I pulled the straps on my seatbelt as tight as I could get them.

The flight attendant pulled the cabin door closed with a thump and the entire plane rocked from the jolt. The motionless propeller on the left wing sputtered to life, spewing thick black smoke as it began to rumble, causing the plane to shake more and vibrate violently.

As we slowly bounced our way down the tarmac, I remember thinking that "this thing was going to fall apart right under our feet"!

The noise of the engines drowned out the flight attendant's announcements and safety instructions that were being issued over the crackling intercom speakers.

I was straining to hear what was being said as I thought to myself, "What difference would it make anyway? After all, if our plane fell out of the sky we would be doomed to die".

Shirley began to pray repeatedly as we braced ourselves for takeoff. I thought to myself, "this is it", as the rickety old plane sped along and lifted off the runway.

A fiercely dreadful sinking feeling in my stomach immediately took over my thoughts. It reminded me of the rush I felt speeding down the highest hill on the Blue Streak roller coaster at the Cedar Point Amusement park when I was a child.

What a rush! In spite of my fear, I couldn't resist looking out the window as we slowly rose higher and higher in the sky leveling off to a mere 10,000 feet or so just above the cloud level.

As we roared through a misty patch into clear skies, an amazing thing was happening. My fear was gone and I realized that I was enjoying this! It felt like the best amusement park ride I had ever been on. The plane was swaying side to side and pitching up and down as we plowed through the air. It felt just like those bumps, thumps and turns on the old, rickety roller coaster tracks.

Peering out the window, I looked down at the city below and thought that it looked just like a circuit board from the inside of a computer or old electronic gadget, reminding me of when I was a kid, destroying old transistor radios. Remember those? I dismantled many things back then just to see what was inside. Funny how things from childhood come back to you isn't it?

By this time my entire body was pumped full of adrenaline and my imagination quickly kicked into high gear as I began to think about all kinds of crazy things. The buildings and roads below me looked like memory chips, resistors and wires. Cars and trucks were like miniature robots moving back and forth.
I wondered what we are really building down there. I thought to myself "this is amazing"! It was just like being in a movie.

Before I knew it, we were on our way down, slinking lower and lower through the air towards the Minneapolis, MN airport.

 The entire flight lasted about 2 hours from lift off to touch down, which, by the way, was actually a really rough, bumpy and shaky ride.

I must have looked like an idiot because I was grinning ear to ear and even laughed with joy as we pitched side to side on our final approach. It was like being on a speed boat breaking the surface of the water every time you jump through a wave. It felt awesome!

We landed with a thump and taxied to the boarding gate quickly. The pilot shut down the engine on the left wing and just like back in Fort Wayne, left the prop on the right wing running. I thought to myself "yea, they would have to jump start this plane if both engines were turned off".

The seatbelt sign was turned off and the flight attendant unbolted the cabin door and thrust it open with a thump. Passengers began to scurry for the door and we followed right along.

As we left the plane, Shirley exclaimed "thank GOD that's over" I smiled (still looking like the cat that caught his first bird) and said "yea, it was really exciting!" She looked bewildered and uttered "uh huh".

For me, that flight is when I reached my turning point, that "aha moment".

I wondered if anyone ever felt the same way I did. Suddenly, everything and everyone around me seemed different. I couldn't wait to get out of the airport to see new things and meet new people. I smiled the whole time and everyone I saw smiled right back. I wished that everyone could feel this way. I wished that I would always feel this way.

It was like being born again, experiencing all the magic and wonders of a childhood adventure. Remember what that felt like?

What simply happened to me that day was the fact that I faced (and defeated) what I perceived to be a significant and imminent danger. My *fear* of flying was magnificently conquered! I now enjoy traveling by plane every chance I get, always looking for a window seat!

This experience was one of the significant critical events that helped me to increase self-confidence, face and overcome many "imaginary barriers" throughout my life and begin the amazing journey towards success!

As you can probably tell by now, I have an active, vivid imagination. Consequently, I have always been able to fabricate all the "worst case scenarios" every time I faced new opportunities.

For some reason, *fear* automatically popped into my mind and as always, it was without any basis of fact.

What is amazing for me is that somehow, I managed to find a way to muster up enough courage to get through many more tough challenges successfully.

Once I realized that something powerful had happened, it forever changed my outlook on life. I knew I had to find out what it was and how it happened.

I chose to seek an understanding of this amazing power. I began my journey to find and reveal the hidden secrets of The Power of Humanity.

To this day, I continue this insatiable quest for knowledge. Along the way, the existence of ancient, primeval forces has been uncovered.

The amazing scientific discoveries of our time were revealed and powerful natural universal laws have been identified.

The results of my findings are here for all to see. These are the ancient secrets that were hidden, protected and kept sacred by powerful rulers throughout the ages. Wars were fought and thousands died in battle to keep these natural powers a secret.

Use them wisely!

The Choices We Make

We were all brought into this world perfectly conceived and innocent. Instantaneously, we have begun the amazing journey of life.

It is my belief that we were exposed to The Power of Humanity before we were even born. In our mothers' womb, our existence and to some extent, our destiny (or our ability to create it) was forming.

Through the course of cosmic time, our genes, chromosomes and DNA have been selectively organized to create powerful divine spiritual beings- Humans. Truly amazing, isn't it?

Right from the start, there is an element of greatness in all of us. At first, it is up to our parents to teach us how to speak, crawl, walk, read, write and hopefully participate productively in society.

Most people would say that it is our parents who teach us the differences between right and wrong. While this is fundamentally true, I firmly believe that we were all endowed with a divine sense of right from wrong at the instant of conception.

In fact, some recent pediatric psychological studies have shown that infants can discern good from evil before they can even say "Mama".

At an early age, we have the power to choose which path we will travel. We are not bound by our family heritage or where we live. We have choices.

I believe this because throughout written history, many amazing people in life came from poor, "dark" family circumstances and yet they somehow managed to emerge to become highly successful, contributing great things to humanity.

Likewise, there are those that came from wealthy, highly successful, "good" families and ended up as drug addicts, thieves or worse. Just read the Hollywood tabloids and you will find evidence for both scenarios.

We all have experienced critical moments in life when something exciting (or tragic) has happened to us or a loved one and had a clear understanding whether it was good or bad. It was the defining moment in our existence when we chose to be positive or negative.

Fortunately for you and me the divine gift of choice is real. It is a powerful and defining human ability and I assume your choice is on the positive side or you probably wouldn't be reading this book!

Stay on this path and you won't be disappointed. Amazing things await you in the future!

I *choose* the word "divine" because it is my belief that there is a Great Ominous Divinity (GOD) at work in the universe and that we are all blessed beyond our comprehension with the ability to contact and access this divinity.

It is my belief that the Great Ominous Divinity (GOD) is a natural phenomenon which has always been and always will be in existence and is freely available for all humanity.

It is also my belief that everything referred to in these pages is abundant everywhere and occurs naturally.

Imagine what you could accomplish with this awesome power at your fingertips!

Here's another amazing phenomenon to ponder. It is my belief that every *choice* we make creates an opportunity for growth.

Two key elements to understand are *"create"* and *"grow"*. Both are naturally occurring every second of every day. It is my belief that no creation can happen without making a choice. Let that soak in for a moment.

Again, I believe that no creation can happen without making choices.

Choices are made up of several elements; thoughts, dreams and intentions. These are the abilities that empower humanity.

This is not a new concept. In fact, it has been known throughout the ages. It is the ancient knowledge that many powerful people don't want others to have. By making a choice we can create success.

Imagine what our world would be like without thoughts and dreams. Nothing would have been created. No electricity, light bulbs, TV, no books, planes, trains, jewelry, medicine, cars, plastic bottles, telephones, space shuttles, computers, ice cream, toothpicks, dental floss, etc. Get the idea? Of course, you do.

It is my belief that we humans are amazingly powerful beings. We can *create* our own environment at will and *choose* to travel on any path we desire. What an awesome power indeed!

For example, imagine *(dream)* you just bought your first house. You searched a long time and finally *chose* the perfect place. Your *dream* home! What's the first thing you need to do? Add your own personal touch right? Create your comfort zone? Make this house a home!

Let's see, what color drapes do you *imagine (dream)* for the master bedroom? Perhaps blue is your favorite color. Do you want a nice floral pattern? Do the walls need a fresh coat of paint? What color do you want? Will you use wall paper or wood paneling?

Choose every aspect of design and use your *imagination*. All you have to do is get the work done and voila! You have *dreamed* and *created* the perfect home to help your family *grow!*

Now that's powerful stuff! It can be applied in every single aspect of your life. You can create your own environment. You possess awesome creative power!

Use your imagination- dream, you will unleash awesome power!

Even though all the power and ability to achieve happiness and success occurs naturally, it does not automatically manifest into our world. We must *choose* to seek, understand and embrace The Power of Humanity.

Those great thinkers and scholars of the ancient world who understood the need for humanity to continue also knew that if they kept this powerful secret to themselves, it would die with them and be lost forever. Fortunately for us, this would not be the case.

Thus, we are blessed with written accounts in our history books, ancient scrolls and even on the walls of the great pyramids. We must never hide these secrets from others as some of the powerful ancient rulers did. To attempt this ultimately leads to a path of destruction.

Today, we are the "keepers" of the great knowledge of the natural Power of Humanity. The Power of Humanity is our birth right. This ancient knowledge belongs to every one of us.

There are many powerful, primeval forces all around us. These too, occur naturally and add to our divinity. We must *choose* to seek them out and set them in motion to fuel our abundant creative power. Tap into these forces and you will be amazed at the results.

It is my belief that we are all divine beings having human experiences and that it is critical for us to focus on our dreams and create an expanding abundance of positive thoughts and energy in order to achieve the amazing happiness and success we deserve.

The choices we make will define and guide us through life. I hope your choice will bring amazing joy and success into your world and those you choose to share it with. Remember, you can create your own environment. Get started now!

The Ancient Secrets

Since the beginning of time, cosmic forces were developing, growing and reacting to create the universe and everything in existence today.

Ever since humans began to think, we began a quest for knowledge. Our thirst for understanding was insatiable. It was never quenched. Even today, question upon question goes unanswered. Millions of people continue to seek the knowledge and understanding of the meaning of life.

How did it begin, where was is it formed, why are we here? These and many, many other questions are asked, studied, researched and tested, over and over, inside and out. Scientists, philosophers, physicists, chemists, biologists, astronomers, scholars, preachers, kings, popes, presidents, knights, crusaders, French, English, Japanese, Germans, Vikings, Arabs, Hebrews, Romans, Aztecs, Mayans and countless other civilizations, all sought to possess the powerful ancient knowledge of the universe.

All throughout the ages, the quest for cosmic power and the search for ancient knowledge that only kings would possess had begun. Rulers would protect and kill for any information that would give them absolute power over people and their kingdoms. They wanted to possess and control the powers of the universe.

Years of research and discoveries were documented, carved into stone, painted on walls and hidden in secret vaults, never to be revealed so that those who possessed the powerful knowledge could rule the world.

They alone would be rich beyond their wildest dreams. They would be the kings that ruled the armies that waged the wars to keep these ancient secrets for themselves. They would die to protect and hide this coveted knowledge.

These are the ancient secrets that were hidden, protected and kept sacred by powerful rulers throughout the ages. Wars were fought and thousands died in battle to keep these powerful secrets hidden from view.

Fortunately for you and me, there were great philosophers, scientists, engineers, teachers and scholars throughout the existence of time that discovered these ancient secrets and understood their importance and sought to reveal them for the benefit of all humankind.

Their understanding of The Power of Humanity was a driving force within them, compelling them to document all that they knew.

They scribbled on cave walls, constructed great monuments, painted miraculous cathedrals, wrote countless texts and passed on their knowledge from generation to generation and this practice still continues in our colleges and laboratories today.

Ancient cultures like the Mayans, Incas, Egyptians and Romans, all left their mark on this earth for us to discover.

Brilliant people like Newton, Leonardo Da Vinci, Michel Nostradamus and Albert Einstein, left their works for us to see.

Modern day scientists like Stephan Hawking and the engineers at NASA put their skills into practice.

Historians and scholars feverishly study their works in a never ending quest to reveal their true meaning and unlock the ancient powers of the universe.

Still, there are powerful people that don't want this great knowledge shared. They want the power for themselves. They want to rule kingdoms and control countries.

Lucky for us, modern technology and instant communication makes it possible for anyone seeking this power to find it and put it to use in their life, achieving great success, abundant health and wealth.

The following pages explain these ancient secrets and how we can use them to expand our knowledge and create prosperity for all humanity.

The Natural Laws of Expansion

As you share your abundant blessings, the Power of Humanity will expand and grow naturally ensuring that our world will be a better place for all humanity.

Natural expansion is the divine element of *growth*. We humans have been growing and expanding our knowledge and power throughout the ages, since the dawn of time. As we were fed, nurtured and cared for, we experienced physical growth. As we learned new things we grew (hopefully) smarter and wiser, experiencing the explosive expansion of our divine species.

Therefore it is my belief that everything in existence must follow the *Natural Laws of Expansion.*

There is a natural phenomenon in the cosmos that applies to everything in existence. Scientists have identified it as dark energy or dark matter. They do not understand it, or have any clue where it comes from. It is an area of great interest and study in today's scientific circles and universities. Physicists refer to its existence as being caused by what they call "spontaneous generation", which basically means it comes from nowhere!

Some speculate that it is a result of the universal "Big Bang" -the theory of evolution. Others hypothesize that it is what actually *caused* the (Big Bang) creation of the universe. You can find reference to this awesome power in many current physics books, as well as in ancient texts.

One thing they all agree with is that it (dark energy) is real and it's *causing the universe to expand!*

It is not a constant, "controlled" expansion. It has also been discovered that the expansion is accelerating! It is moving faster and faster always expanding, in every direction, always accelerating- Naturally.

This natural force (dark energy) that is causing the expansion is also growing everywhere in the cosmos, faster and faster! Consequently, this powerful force is causing everything in existence everywhere to expand and move faster.

It is my belief that this mysterious energy is the result of physical displacement caused by natural growth. As growth occurs, it takes up more space and consequently displaces the surrounding space, pushing it outward.

New planets are constantly appearing, new galaxies are being formed. Just look at our own existence- life is expanding every second, displacing the space on earth.

To me, this perfectly explains why it is spontaneously expanding, getting stronger and stronger, seemingly coming from "nowhere".

This natural expansion is fueled by growth and touches every thought, every dream, every choice, every movement, every element and molecule and everything in existence everywhere all the way down to the atomic level! Imagine that! Everything is expanding naturally!

I have been able to understand, accept and embrace this natural force of expansion into my life. Because of it, my world has changed and it is getting better and better. My personal life has improved, my joy is abundant. I have success at work, at play and in every goal I set.

The good news is that you too can experience these awesome transformations. My hope is that after reading this book, you will understand (or at least believe it exists) this Ominous Divine Power and begin to enjoy the rewards of abundant expansion every day.

Think about it. If the world around you is always affected by the Natural Laws of Expansion, then you must be also. Most assuredly, you are! Hopefully, you are able to recognize it.

There's nothing you or I can do to stop it. The Natural Laws of Expansion are at work for everyone everyday and in everyway, naturally! Use it to realize your dreams. Start now and put something, anything into motion!

I believe that we all have the ability to tap into the Natural Laws of Expansion and when we do, we'll become stronger, healthier, wealthier, smarter, and happier.

Beware! There is a fundamental element of the Natural Laws of Expansion. Because it is abundantly available and occurs naturally, this power works indiscriminately for positive or negative. Because it is natural, it does not separate evil from good, black from white, old from young, boy from girl, etc.

This, I believe, is why there are terrible atrocities in our world, side by side with awesome blessings. It is also why some people become depressed while devastating misery continues to pile up in their lives. The more they focus on the negative, the faster it continues to expand! Don't get caught up in this spiral! Keep positive energy working for you at all times!

For example, if someone sits around and dwells on negative thoughts all day, every day, in no time at all, they will become increasingly weak and depressed. They will become physically ill and begin to decay. They will likely get sicker, grow weaker and continue to get deeper into depression.

Despair will naturally expand and "bad things" will constantly happen to them. They will lose the spark to dream and they will ultimately rot and die.

Do not focus on negative thoughts! Your wish (dream) will be realized beyond your expectations growing worse and worse, naturally!

The point is that you must choose to deny negativity a place in your life. No matter what circumstances you may face, the power to change them is within you. Use the Natural Laws of Expansion to transform your life.

The old cliché "use it or lose it" is actually an ancient instruction explaining how to tap into the Natural Laws of Expansion, which happens to be active all of the time everywhere, in everyone's life.

You can't turn it off because it is spontaneous. This awesome divine power is at work in our lives 24/7 and there's nothing we can do to stop it, like or not.

The one thing we can do is change our thoughts. No matter how bad things may seem we all have the ability to tap into the Power of Humanity and use the Natural Laws of Expansion to turn things around!

Do you want a life of excitement, success and happiness? Your wish (dream) will be realized. It will be an amazing life beyond your expectations. You will enjoy abundant happiness and success. And it will continue to grow- naturally!

The key to success is that we have to make a choice. We have to move, change directions head to the positive side. We have to use our divine power and have faith that better days are ahead. We have to want (desire) a better life and must be willing to do whatever it takes to get there.

We must embrace the Power of Humanity, be relentless in generating positive thoughts while deliberately maintaining a positive attitude and put the Natural Laws of Expansion into motion.

Focus on your dreams for success! Make choices. Take action. The smallest effort will grow. The largest efforts will grow. They must grow because it is natural for it to happen!

The only thing that is holding you back and hindering you from creating and realizing your dreams is you!

Put the Laws of Expansion in motion. Say these words out loud to yourself every day, "I am happy, healthy, wealthy and wise. I can and will achieve my goals" Start today!

Remember you have to use it or lose it! The Natural Laws of Expansion are in force right now!

Use It or Lose It

You've heard of the term "Karma" right? You know the old cliché, "what goes around comes around", or "you get back what you give". Guess what- This is real!

It is a natural, powerful occurrence in the universe. Just like the Natural Laws of Expansion, there's nothing you or I can do to stop it. This amazing force has always been and always will be active in everything that exists!

The more you give, the more you get. The more you save, the more you earn. The more you learn, the more you know. Natural expansion and spontaneous generation of "dark energy" also affects Karma!

Let's explore this concept.

It is my belief that everything in existence is naturally orbital. I'll say it again. Everything in existence is naturally *orbital*. All the way down to the atomic level.

Everything that goes around will eventually come back around. It has to, because of the orbital laws of Karma.

Remember your science tests? Everything is made up of molecules, which all contain atoms which all have electrons orbiting around them. That's right, *orbiting!*

Therefore, I conclude that it is natural for everything that we put into motion to return back to us and because the Natural Laws of Expansion are in play, it will come back to us faster and stronger than when we started! Wow!

This is critical for us to understand! The only influence we can hope to have is our focused positive thoughts. Make sure to keep this concept working for you at all times.

You'll be amazed with the results from your efforts. A return on your "investment" is naturally guaranteed!

It is elementary for me to point out that as far as we humans know, nothing exists anywhere without a balance of positive and negative, Yin and Yang. Even atomically, it is required to have an Electron (positive) and a Neutron (negative).

So this means good and bad, positive and negative, must (and do) occur naturally and exist in everything everywhere.

All of the ancient prophets, powerful rulers and great thinkers throughout history figured this out too.

This is why our world is the way it is today. This is why we have such amazing technology at our fingertips.

It has been recorded by ancient Greeks, Romans & Egyptians to modern day inventors. Even the Holy Bible indicates that Jesus knew the Power of Humanity and how to use it. He knew about karma.

Could this be why the "golden rule" was created in the first place and what its purpose is? Remember the words?

"Do unto others as you would have them do unto you"

I say without any question, yes! Jesus was deliberately and purposefully setting the orbital laws of Karma into motion for the benefit of all humanity!

Believe me when I say that karma is real and that it absolutely is happening naturally and due to the Natural Laws of Expansion, it is growing and moving faster and faster. Your deeds will definitely come back to you.

You now have the basics of this awesome, coveted, secret ancient knowledge. We humans have the power to shape our destiny. Everything we do can and will come back to us. And because of the Natural Laws of Expansion, it will grow and come back stronger!

You absolutely will get back what you give. Be sure to give your best effort in every task. Be sure to focus enthusiastic (positive) energy into every thought.

Choose wisely because you will get the dream you create and there's nothing you can do to stop it, once it is set into motion.

What will you do with this awesome, powerful knowledge?

I trust that you will USE IT OR LOSE IT!

Every day I am grateful for the great ominous divinity (GOD) and the fact that we are blessed with the Power of Humanity! Our ability to choose up or down, left or right, good or evil, affords us the freedom to achieve anything we want.

Remember to be careful what you wish for! You will most assuredly receive it, naturally. Choose your thoughts and dreams carefully.

The Natural Laws of Expansion and Karma are at work every day, all around us, all of the time, right this instant!

Are you skeptical? Do you need proof? Here's where things start to get exciting! Don't just blindly trust what I say, go and do some research for yourself! You will find evidence in one form or another that irrefutably supports my discoveries.

You can try simple experiments on your own to prove the elements of the power of humanity are working in your life.

Let's begin by choosing something simple to test my claims. When you see the result, you will want more. When you want more you will begin to think (dream) about what you desire.

The Natural Laws of Expansion and Karma will begin to work and when it comes back around in orbit, you will be amazed how easy it was and how much it grew!

Remember to allow some time for things to develop. The key is that you have to do something and you must expect results. If you don't, it's likely you'll miss the miraculous event! It will happen even if you don't realize it and your circumstances will be changed and hopefully improved.

You have control over how you feel. You have control over how you act and react. No one can be responsible for your actions but you. You alone are accountable for how you participate in life.

Every action results in a consequence, no matter how small. You may never see the result but it will happen and at some point it will come back to you in some way, shape or form.

Make sure it is in line with your wishes by sending only positive energy. It may be money, a new job, a promotion or prize, maybe it's the approval for the mortgage you're hoping for. Whatever it is, be sure to look for it and recognize that it is a direct result from your use of The Power of Humanity.

The first step on this journey is to change the way you think and the things you think about. It is essential for you to open your mind to the idea that you can control your destiny and set actions in motion today that will affect your life in the future. You have to have faith that your life will change even if you don't see results immediately.

Here's a simple exercise for you to test my theory and discover The Power of Humanity for yourself. This is an exercise in human influence.

You will need to select someone you don't know personally. It may be the bus driver you see every day, the Starbuck's counter person that takes your morning coffee money or perhaps someone at your work or school.

Day in and day out, there is little eye contact with this person and rarely, if any, acknowledgement that either of you exist, even though your paths cross daily.

Start right now (make it a Monday) and every day (just for 5 days) look that person in the eye and simply smile and say hello. No additional conversation is required, unless by some miracle you get a smile back (Karma) with a hello as well! Your human power will affect this person.

Even if that person does not respond in kind at first, just move on with your day. Be sure to do it again the next day. You must do this for 5 consecutive days without fail.

It won't hurt and it doesn't take any additional effort on your part since you see this person every day anyway. You have to stick it out consistently for at least five days, no less.

While doing this experiment, keep in mind that any person you meet today may be the person that you need help from tomorrow. Remember that Karma is real and what goes around will definitely come back around, naturally.

Next, every time someone asks you how you are, answer with "I am fabulous" or "I am awesome" or any positive statement that you feel comfortable with.

Make a deliberate effort to proclaim you are having a great day just because you woke up.

Do this no matter how you are truly feeling. Continue this positive affirmation without fail, each and every day.

During this time, pay attention to how you actually feel. In a small way, it begins to make you feel good. In fact you will find yourself in a better mood which, in turn will affect your entire day, your family, coworkers and all others around you.

You will begin to see firsthand The Power of Humanity in action. I am positive that your day will be better than it was yesterday. You will get more done and your job will begin to feel important. Your boss will notice your positive energy and make note of it. People will want to be around you because you make them feel good!

You may not be able to pinpoint why at first, but you will know for sure something is different and somehow better. Naturally, you will want more. Naturally, you will receive more because the orbital forces of Karma and the Natural Laws of Expansion are always occurring in the universe and in your life.

Practice applying the "golden rule" and do for others what you would have them do for you.

This is your second chance! Continue your days with deliberate enthusiasm and you'll begin using the Power of Humanity. Naturally, it will grow within you and expand your joy, increasing your success, growing faster and faster as the days go by.

Remember you must "use it or lose it"! Once you see this divine power manifest into your life, it will open doors that you never knew existed. Be sure to walk through them!

The Power of Humanity will offer you a second chance. It will lead you to a new way of living, a new purpose, an understanding of who you are, where you want to go and how you are going to get there.

This simple exercise was the turning point for me. Once I was able to see the Power of Humanity working in my life, I knew I had changed. I knew there was a better way of life and that the possibilities were endless! I realized that the Natural Laws of Expansion, fueled by Karma were active and that second chances are real!

Second Chances Are Real

We only have one life to live but have many chances to change direction anytime we choose and make our lives better. Believe me when I say second chances are real! They are very real and available to all of us anytime.

Each day that you wake up can offer that second chance. Look for it, seek it and you will find it! With The Power of Humanity at your fingertips, the Natural Laws of Expansion and Karma at work, there's no limit to the possibilities!

Like many people, I struggled hopelessly for years. I was always a winner I just didn't know it until I discovered these natural principles.

I have a second chance to create the life I've always dreamed of and I'm working on it every day! You can too!

It is essential for you to know if you are happy where you're headed today. Think about it. If the answer is no, then you're in luck because there is another chance for happiness!

Believe me when I tell you there are endless opportunities to turn your life around. Karma is at work and ultimately will pay you a visit whether you want it, or not.

You do have to exert some effort and try a different approach to alter your situation but you can do it because you have the natural ability at your command and the promise that second chances are real!

Focus on understanding your circumstances. No matter how difficult they are, a solution to improve is at your fingertips. If you have a true desire to change, you will and when you do, it will be like an amazing miracle!

Make a choice to do the "right thing" the next time you face a problem. It will set you on a path to incredible success!

When work is done with integrity, the value is clear and always rewarded. Karma will see to that!

If stress overwhelms your morning, take a deep breath and change course immediately. Head toward success & happiness! It is easier said than done but doable nonetheless.

You must deliberately get focused on all positive aspects in your life. This practice will help relieve the stress and set you on the right track again.

Choose only positive thoughts and dismiss all negative energy. No matter what is happening in your life there are good things around you. Do not let any depressing thought cloud your memory.

The first thing you do after waking up will set your day in motion. Look in the mirror and say out loud "Today will be a great day" "I am happy, healthy, wealthy and wise". Speaking these words will have a powerful effect on the day's events.

Whether you believe it, or not, a second chance will be created. You will have a better day.

There will always be a second chance because you are a powerful being with the ability to make choices!

Be sure to look for it!

The Power of Humanity occurs naturally within all of us we need only to think about it clearly and a powerful change will happen, naturally!

When you look back at all the re-dos and second chances throughout your life it will become as clear to you as it is for me.

You can always turn things around no matter what the circumstances are. This is possible because of second chances. Not only are they real and abundant, they occur naturally, thanks to the Power of Humanity!

Second chances naturally happen automatically. Look for them every time you make a mistake or feel regret.

If you open your mind to alternatives you'll have a clear vision of what to change. Think about how to do it over and then implement your choices.

Like magic, your second chance will materialize. It's not magic. It is the natural Power of Humanity and you are putting it to use in your life.

Make sure you deliberately seek continuous improvement in your life, continuous improvement in your career and continuous improvement in every aspect of your dreams.

Focus on improving your circumstances. No matter how difficult they are, a solution to make things better is at your fingertips.

Seek out answers and you will find another way, a second chance. This is what learning from your mistakes is all about. This will help you improve.

It's a natural phenomenon working continuously for you. Second chances are real, abundant and available for you 24 hours a day 7 days a week for your entire life. They were always there and always will be.

There is a never ending supply of powerful opportunities. Take advantage of this power every chance you can and in every way you can imagine.

You must remember that it is OK to make mistakes. You could not have learned to use second chances without having made some mistakes.

You would not be able to get anywhere if you allow the *fear* of messing up to get in your way.

Regrets are good sources of power. It is always better to acknowledge a mistake than to wonder what might have been.

Did you ever say to yourself "I'll never do that again" or "I wish I had done that"? I'll bet the answer is yes. Good for you! You understand that second chances exist!

I say, "It is better to know the result than to wonder what might have been".

These are second chances at work right in front of you! Right under your nose! Take a chance, make another choice, change your mind, try and try again. You won't be disappointed and if you are, use another second chance until you get it right!

Are you getting this? No matter what you do second chances are available. If you look for them you will find them. Don't ever give up or you will lose them.

Lost time can never be found and lost opportunities will disappear as well. Taking no action will grow to negative results. Karma will make sure of it!

It is important to remember that when you wonder what might have been if you had made different choices you began a cycle.

Try again in a different way. You'll be amazed at the result. This is how to put the second chance power into motion.

The old clichés are proof of this ancient truth, "If at first, you don't succeed, try, try again" and the ever familiar "practice makes perfect".

It's been known throughout the centuries and is still true today, second chances are real. They are natural occurrences and are available to all of us!

Pay attention to everything and everyone around you. Eventually, you will begin to see and grasp the infinite pool of second chances. Put them to work now!

When you are clear and focused on results, another amazing thing will happen. You will begin to experience an unfamiliar confidence. Old *fears* will vanish. You will begin to feel powerful and everyone around you will begin to react differently.

You will be transformed into a leader. Use this newly discovered power carefully! Great responsibility and accountability will reside with you.

Positive energy will begin to surround you and attract positive people and positive forces. Change will begin to overwhelm your life. Karma has come around as you knew it would, giving back with increased energy.

This is the time to keep a keen eye on your dreams. This is the critical turning point when you will begin to feel, understand and use the Power of Humanity for the rest of your life.

This is your second chance! Use it to help others. Share it with your loved ones! You will not regret it and karma will be back with greater blessings the next time around.

You must always strive to remember that the Natural Laws of Expansion, karma and the spoken words of The Power of Humanity are at your command!

Never give up, never quit and you will be **ABLE** to succeed beyond your wildest dreams!

Be ABLE to Use the Power

There are many elements that make up the Power of Humanity. In order to enjoy the full natural empowerments of humanity we must be *ABLE* to receive them and be worthy of the inevitable consequences from their use.

The word **ABLE** that I refer to in this chapter is an acronym for a set of ancient instructions for conjuring up the coveted ancient secret knowledge that leads to use of The Power of Humanity.

These are the instructions that were protected as ancient secrets which have been hidden in plain sight and written for all humanity to see since the dawn of time. The instructions are specific commands that will empower humanity and guarantee amazing success and prosperity for all who believe and embrace them as truth.

Ask and you shall receive (seek and ye shall find) help, knowledge and guidance.

Believe in yourself (have faith) you must know who you are.

Live for the moment (act like you're already there) and make every second count.

Expect the absolute best (look for results)

Do any of these sound familiar to you? They should. As I said, they have all been hidden in plain sight and written for anyone to see. They have been printed in ancient books, such as the Holy Bible, chiseled into stone tablets and scribed onto papyrus scrolls throughout man's existence.

They have been coveted by kings, sought after by crusaders and guarded by secret societies throughout the ages.

They are powerful instructions and incantations used to evoke divine power. Now that you know these secrets you can begin to use them every day. Once mastered, you will possess these powerful ancient secrets and be **ABLE** to accept and use the Power of Humanity!

Now is the time to start the cycle and create an image, dream or wish. Seek or *ask* for what you want. Dream big! Your wish will start the cycle.

Imagine being where you have always dreamed to be. You must be sure to keep your dreams grounded in reality. You can achieve wealth but you will never ride a fire breathing dragon.

When you create a clear picture in your mind of what success is to you, you will be *able* (there's that word again) to begin your journey and achieve your goals.

Start with the first powerful instruction and *ask* for what you want. Every night before you go to sleep, focus all of your thoughts on what you want to achieve in the future. Be as specific as possible. Do you want to be wealthy? How much money do you need? Do you want to be the president of your company? Do you want a better relationship with loved ones?

Focus your thoughts with all of your energy. Do this every night until you see a clear picture of yourself as if that dream was real, then wish (ask) for an understanding of what you will need to do to reach your goal.

Ask others for help. Find an expert in the field you seek to champion. Seek knowledge in any form you can find. Use books, magazines or internet to feed your knowledge. The more you learn, the sooner you will realize your dreams.

Before you can even recognize any progress you will already have traveled closer to your destiny. You will be astonished by your new energy and accomplishments. The Natural Laws of Expansion will respond, set Karma into motion and you will be amazed even more.

You will be on your way to realizing your dream without even noticing it! It will be manifesting into reality automatically, because of the Natural Laws of Expansion and orbital forces of Karma.

Once you start using these ancient secrets, natural expansion kicks in and propels the inevitable success you desire! And get this- once in motion, you will not be able to stop it! It will happen (as it has to) because it is naturally occurring due to the divine power you evoked.

Keep in mind many great things take time to build. Results may not happen overnight. Stay focused. You must be **ABLE** to see your progress.

You also possess the natural ability to effect change. That's the beauty of it all! You get another chance to do something different. By now you can see what I mean and how second chances are real, and when you make yourself available, you are **ABLE** to reap amazing benefits from the Power of Humanity.

Ask yourself if the chosen path will lead to your dream. Seek guidance from within. Focus every night before falling to sleep. The Power of Humanity holds the answer and you will ultimately know what you need to do.

Believe your instincts and *believe* in your dreams. You must have confidence in your ability to achieve your dreams and goals. You have chosen to seek success. Have faith that the cycle has been started and that you are the only one who has control of the outcome.

Never let anyone convince you that it can't be done. You must not accept defeat ever, especially when you haven't even begun the journey. Others will not and cannot see your future as you can. Even loved ones may not offer support to your cause. Stay focused.

You must *believe* that you will reach your destiny. Have faith in your determination for success. Have faith that the Power of Humanity is real and that the Natural Laws of Expansion and Karma are powerful forces that you have set into motion. You will not be disappointed.

It is the *belief* in your ideas and dreams that will fuel your desire to drive these awesome forces and create your success. You must convince your mind that these dreams can come true. Every night you have to think about where you are and where you want to be. Practice visualizing yourself already achieving the goal.

This "self-programming" is a key element for locking-in the true *belief* deep into your soul. Once accomplished, there's no stopping your inevitable success!

Practice every night before you drift off to sleep. Say to yourself "I am a powerful being", "I am successful at------", "I will achieve-------"(you fill in the blanks). Be specific and think big. Set your dreams into motion and use the natural forces available to bring them into reality. Practice, practice and practice!

Believe you have already achieved great things, that you now possess the ability to use the Powers of Humanity in your life. Do this every night without fail until it becomes natural and routine.

Now that the natural forces of nature and The Power of Humanity have manifested into your life you must be ready to accept the abundant blessings heading your way. You have to *"live* like you're already there".

Certainly by now you have been energized with a feeling of confidence, knowing that you are on your way to glorious accomplishments! Now you must act like it. You must "be" your dream.

Proclaim your dream to people that can help you along the way. Proclaim to yourself every conscious moment you can. Look in the mirror and see yourself as a confident successful champion. Convince yourself into success. Act like you are already there.

You must now begin to *live* like you have achieved your dreams. You have to" *live* for the moment". Mold every second into the final masterpiece.

For example, if your self-proclaimed dream is to be the president and CEO of a successful company you should act like it. You should dress like you are the CEO. What does a successful executive look like? Start transforming your image immediately. Believe me when I say nobody will take you seriously if you look like someone who just spent the night sleeping on a park bench!

Study your current situation. What's it going to take for you to get there? Make a list. Study every aspect you can imagine that will help you create your dream.

Don't waste any valuable time worrying about the challenges ahead. *Fear* will stop you dead in your tracks.

Hold your head high knowing that you control your destiny and are on your way to realizing your dreams! Just *live* in the moment. Today is when you can do something positive, tomorrow isn't here yet.

Start moving now.

Write your thoughts down on paper. Make a list. It can be short or long it makes no difference. You will need a roadmap to plan your journey. Even if today you don't have a clue where to start, the answers will come. Just write something down on paper relating to your dream. Even a simple statement such as "I am a successful-----" (you fill in the gap) will start the process. Do it now.

You will be ABLE to reach your dreams as long as you follow these guidelines. It will happen in spite of your *fears* because it is natural to do so. *Live* in the moment! Make every second count.

Produce something, anything pertaining to your dream at every opportunity possible. Now is a good time! Tiny, seemingly insignificant activities will yield huge benefits in the future. They must and will because of the Natural Laws of Expansion and the forces of Karma!

Live like you're already there, act like the person you want others to see. Become your dream.

Expect the absolute best in everything you do and from everything under your control. Every second counts. Lost or wasted time cannot be recovered it is guaranteed to be lost forever.

This is why you must be focused on achieving your goals at all times in every way, every day without exception.

No matter what task is being done, make sure it is done with 100% quality. You must always *expe*ct the absolute best from yourself. Never let mediocre, lazy work slip into your life. It will feed the wrong energy and it too will expand naturally. Less than perfect is your enemy!

Although as humans we make mistakes we must strive for perfection in every aspect of our lives. If we accept less, that is what we will get. And that will alter the path to your destiny naturally.

If you think you need to make a change, do it! After all, second chances are there for us to use freely and help us reach our goals!

We must be **ABLE** to imagine our success and be ready to do what it takes to achieve our goals.

Focus on being the best at what you do. No matter what the job is, do it as if no one else can do it better than you.

Expect and deliver the absolute best.

If you are sweeping the floor, be sure there's not even a speck of dust left when you're finished. Make sure every detail is considered and that there is no stone left unturned. This is the proven path to success!

The orbital forces of Karma and the Natural Laws of Expansion will thrust you into hyper-speed towards achieving success beyond your wildest dreams!

Now that you know what these coveted powerful ancient secrets are, make sure you use them! You now possess the ancient secret knowledge that has been sought after by great rulers and fought for by knights, crusaders and warriors on their relentless quests for power and glory throughout history.

Now you too, have the divine knowledge of the Power of Humanity, the orbital laws of Karma and the Natural Laws of Expansion. Don't let this awesome power sit idle. Put it to use in your life now!

If you don't know what you really want, make a wish list. Dream big and write down your wildest desires. This is the easiest and necessary first step toward your success!

Remember that it is essential for you to focus all thoughts for your vision of the future. You control your dreams. Practice every night without fail to put all of the natural laws into motion, working for you.

Use your natural power and regenerate tonight. Tune in to your thoughts of success. Control your dreams by using repetitive statements.

Focus on abundant health and energy. Wish for wealth and prosperity, dream about peace and happiness.

Evoke the divine power within you and seek The Power of Humanity. You have awesome power at your fingertips as long as you are willing and **ABLE** to accept it.

Ask and you shall receive (seek and ye shall find) help, knowledge and guidance.

Believe in yourself (have faith) you must know who you are.

Live for the moment (act like you're already there) and make every second count.

Expect the absolute best (look for results)

Words of Wisdom from the Masters

A collection of quotes from our world's philosophers, thinkers, masters and champions

The controlled person is a powerful person. He who always keeps his head will get ahead. -Norman V. Peale

Good actions give strength to ourselves & inspire good actions in others. -Plato

If your actions inspire others to dream more, learn more, do more and become more, you are a leader. -John Quincy Adams

You're never beaten until you admit it. -George S. Patton

Be not afraid of going slow. Be afraid only of standing still. -Chinese Proverb

The great question is not whether you have failed, but whether you are content with failure. -Chinese Proverb

The less routine, the more exciting is life.

-Amos Bronson Alcott

We are what we repeatedly do. Excellence then, is not an act, but a habit. -Aristotle

Your words, thoughts and dreams have amazing creative power! Use them wisely. -Thomas E. Montagu

Teachers open the door but you must walk through it yourself. - Chinese Proverb

What it lies in our power to do, it lies in our power not to do. -Aristotle

Keep a watch on your behavior; make sure all your ways are rightly ordered. -Proverbs 4:26

We make a living by what we get. We make a life by what we give. -Winston Churchill

No problem can be solved from the same level of consciousness that created it. -Albert Einstein

It is difficult to defeat those who would insist on victory.

-Chinese Proverb

An honest answer is like a kiss on the lips, full of passion. -Proverbs 24:26

The beginning of wisdom is to call things by their right names. -Chinese Proverb

The journey is the reward. -Chinese Proverb

Good habits formed at youth make all the difference.

-Aristotle

Once you pour the water out of the bucket it's hard to get it back in it. -Chinese Proverb

Sow much, reap much; sow little, reap little.

-Chinese Proverb

Choose a job you love, & you will never have to work a day in your life. -Confucius

A person that never made any mistakes, never really tried anything new. -Albert Einstein

Health and good estate of body are above all gold. A strong body is above infinite wealth. -Ecclesiastics 30:15

When we have nothing to worry about we are not doing much, & not doing much may supply us with plenty of future worries. -Chinese Proverb

Everything has its beauty but not everyone sees it.

-Confucius

Those who wish to sing, always find a song.

-Swedish Proverb

He who asks the question is a fool for a minute; he who does not is a fool forever. -Chinese Proverb

A brave man dies once, a coward a thousand times.

-African Proverb

A gem cannot be polished without friction, nor a man perfected without trials. -Chinese Proverb

By nature, men are nearly alike; by practice, they get to be wide apart. -Confucius

Be as you wish to seem. -Socrates

The greatest virtues are those which are most useful to other people. -Aristotle

A heart that loves is always young. -Greek Proverb

The more a man meditates upon good thoughts the better will be his world & the world at large. - Confucius

Idleness is the mother of all vices. -Russian Proverb

It is never too late to be what you might have been.

-George Eliot

A man grows most tired while standing still.

-Chinese Proverb

You will never know what you're good at until you try.

-Chinese Proverb

The human capacity to care for others isn't something trivial or something to be taken for granted. Rather it is something we should cherish. -Dalai Lama

No act of kindness, no matter how small, is ever wasted.

 -Aesop

Pleasure in the job puts perfection in the work. -Aristotle

If you damage the character of another, you damage your own. -African Proverb

Learning is a treasure that will follow its owner everywhere. -Chinese Proverb

In the end, it's not the years in your life that count. It's the life in your years. -Abraham Lincoln

Do unto others as you would have them do unto you.
-Jesus Christ

Finally, always remember;

There is awesome power in our universe that can be accessed by anyone, anytime, anywhere.

All we have to do is understand what it is and how to tap into it. We must be **ABLE** -then we can begin using these amazing, natural forces to enrich our human experience.

The Power of Humanity, fueled by the Natural Laws of Expansion and orbital effects of Karma, is our divine ability to love, choose, think, dream and create.

– Thomas E. Montagu

IT'S NEVER TOO LATE FOR CHANGE!

Thomas E Montagu
7/11/2018

Made in the USA
Columbia, SC
25 June 2018